CHECKERBOARD BIOGRAPHY LIBRARY
U.S. PRESIDENTS

The
United States Presidents

GEORGE WASHINGTON

ABDO Publishing Company

Tamara L. Britton

visit us at
www.abdopublishing.com

Published by ABDO Publishing Company, 8000 West 78th Street, Edina, Minnesota 55439.
Copyright © 2009 by Abdo Consulting Group, Inc. International copyrights reserved in all countries.
No part of this book may be reproduced in any form without written permission from the publisher.
The Checkerboard Library™ is a trademark and logo of ABDO Publishing Company.

Printed in the United States.

Cover Photo: Corbis
Interior Photos: Alamy p. 18; AP Images pp. 5, 23, 25, 29; Corbis p. 27; (c) 2008 the George
     Washington Foundation p. 9; Getty Images p. 14; iStockphoto p. 32; Library of Congress pp. 12,
     13, 15, 17, 21; National Archives pp. 19, 22, 24; Picture History p. 11

Editor: BreAnn Rumsch
Art Direction & Cover Design: Neil Klinepier
Interior Design: Jaime Martens

Library of Congress Cataloging-in-Publication Data

Britton, Tamara L., 1963-
 George Washington / Tamara L. Britton.
    p. cm. -- (The United States presidents)
 Includes index.
 ISBN 978-1-60453-479-5
 1. Washington, George, 1732-1799--Juvenile literature. 2. Presidents--United States--Biography--
Juvenile literature. I. Title.

 E312.66.B69 2009
 973.4'1092--dc22
 [B]
                              2008033505

CONTENTS

GEORGE WASHINGTON

George Washington is one of the United States's most important presidents. He was born in Virginia before it was a state. In fact, the United States did not yet exist. When Washington was a boy, Virginia was a British colony.

Growing up, Washington liked to play in the woods near his home. Later he became a **surveyor**. When Washington was 20 years old, he joined the military. He fought in the **French and Indian War**.

In 1758, Washington was elected to the Virginia House of **Burgesses**. He also managed Mount Vernon, his large plantation. The next year, he married Martha Dandridge Custis.

When Great Britain began to tax the colonists unfairly, they declared their independence. Washington led the colonists to victory in the **American Revolution**. Then, the United States became an independent country. Because of his leadership, Washington was elected the country's first president.

TIMELINE

1732 - George Washington was born on February 22, at Pope's Creek in Virginia Colony.

1749 - Washington was named surveyor of Culpepper County.

1752 - Washington became a major in the Virginia army.

1754 - On May 28, Washington's army defeated the French in the Battle of Jumonville Glen; on July 3 the French defeated Washington's army in the Battle of Great Meadows.

1755 - Washington assisted General Edward Braddock in the Battle of the Monongahela on July 9; Washington was named commander of Virginia's troops in August.

1758 - Washington was elected to the Virginia House of Burgesses.

1759 - On January 6, Washington married Martha Dandridge Custis.

1774 - Washington attended the First Continental Congress in September.

1775 - In May, Washington attended the Second Continental Congress; Washington was chosen to lead the Continental army.

1776 - The Declaration of Independence was signed on July 4; on December 25, Washington led his men across the Delaware River in the American Revolution.

1781 - French soldiers helped the Continental army win the Battle of Yorktown.

1783 - On September 3, the British and the colonists signed the Treaty of Paris.

1787 - Washington and other state leaders attended the Constitutional Convention.

1789 - On April 30, Washington was inaugurated as the nation's first president.

1792 - President Washington was elected to a second term.

1799 - George Washington died on December 14.

When George Washington was born, England's North American colonies used the Julian calendar. On that calendar, Washington's birthday was February 11. England and its colonies adopted the Gregorian calendar in 1752. Then, February 11 became February 22.

When Washington was elected president, he received every electoral vote. No other president since then has received every electoral vote.

Washington's second inaugural address is the shortest ever given. It was just 135 words long.

Every U.S. president has lived in the White House except President Washington.

PRESIDENT OF THE
POTUS
UNITED STATES

YOUNG GEORGE

George Washington was born on February 22, 1732, at Pope's Creek in Virginia Colony. Virginia Colony was one of Great Britain's North American settlements.

George was the first of Augustine and Mary Washington's six children. George also had two half brothers from his father's first marriage. He was especially close to his half brother Lawrence. Lawrence was a **cultivated** gentleman. He became George's role model and **mentor**.

When George was three years old, his family moved to Little Hunting Creek Farm. The farm was near the Potomac River. There, George explored the woods and helped out on the farm. In 1738, the family moved to nearby Ferry Farm. In 1743, George's father died. George continued to live at Ferry Farm with his mother and siblings for several years.

FAST FACTS

BORN - February 22, 1732

WIFE - Martha Dandridge Custis (1731–1802)

CHILDREN - 2 stepchildren

POLITICAL PARTY - None

AGE AT INAUGURATION - 57

YEARS SERVED - 1789–1797

VICE PRESIDENT - John Adams

DIED - December 14, 1799, age 67

On July 2, 2008, the George Washington Foundation announced the discovery of the remains of Washington's home at Ferry Farm. Archaeologists have unearthed thousands of artifacts from the site.

A teapot lid from the 1700s

Curlers used to curl wigs

Part of a stoneware mug fragment showing Great Britain's King George III

Lawrence owned a large estate called Mount Vernon. He lived there with his wife, Anne Fairfax. Anne came from an important family. Her father, Lord Fairfax, helped George get a good job. In 1749, George was named **surveyor** of Culpepper County.

In 1751, Lawrence became ill. He and George traveled to Barbados, a warm tropical island. Lawrence thought the climate there might help him recover. But he died the next year. In his **will**, Lawrence left Mount Vernon to his wife. After she died, the estate would belong to George.

MILITARY MAN

Lawrence had once served in Virginia's army. Washington decided to join the army, too. When he was 20, Washington became a major. It was not long before his service was needed.

Like Britain, France had settlements in North America. The French army had built forts on land claimed by the British. Virginia governor Robert Dinwiddie wrote a letter that said the British owned the land. He sent Washington to deliver the letter to the French. But the French would not leave.

In 1754, Dinwiddie again sent Washington to make Britain's claim to the lands. On May 28, Washington's army attacked a French force. Several men were killed in the Battle of Jumonville Glen. This battle started the **French and Indian War**.

Washington retreated and built Fort Necessity for protection. The French attacked the fort on July 3 in the Battle of Great Meadows. This time, Washington was forced to surrender.

The next year, the British sent General Edward Braddock to defeat the French and secure Britain's lands. Washington went along as Braddock's assistant. The army set out through the wilderness to confront the French in present-day Pennsylvania.

In addition to the loss of General Braddock, 900 soldiers were killed in the battle.

But the British soldiers were not used to fighting in the woods. They marched out in the open where the enemy could see them. On July 9, 1755, Native Americans and French soldiers **ambushed** the British army. In the Battle of the Monongahela, Braddock's troops were defeated, and he was killed.

Washington fought gallantly. He led the surviving soldiers to safety. Because of his actions, Washington was promoted to colonel. Then in August, he was named commander of Virginia's troops.

In 1758, the British secured the land. Washington resigned from the army. That same year, he was elected to the Virginia House of **Burgesses**.

SUCCESSFUL PLANTER

On January 6, 1759, Washington married a widow named Martha Dandridge Custis. Martha had a son named Jack. She had a daughter who was also named Martha. Everyone called her Patsy. The Washingtons lived at Mount Vernon.

Mount Vernon was a plantation. Hundreds of slaves worked there. Some slaves worked in the house as cooks or as maids. Some were millers and **coopers**. Others were blacksmiths and carpenters. Slaves wove cloth and made clothing and shoes. However, most worked in the fields tending crops.

At first, Washington grew mostly tobacco. Later, he added other crops, such as corn and wheat. He experimented with crop rotation and tried different fertilizers to increase his harvests. Washington wanted to make Mount Vernon more profitable.

WASHINGTON & SLAVERY

In George Washington's time, slavery was legal. But, Washington questioned slavery in a land of freedom and liberty. In his will, Washington said his slaves were to be freed after his wife, Martha, died.

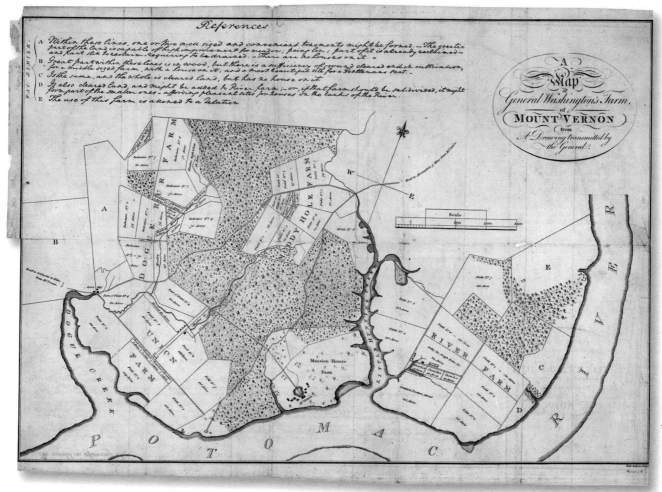

Washington surveyed Mount Vernon and drew this map of the property.

But, Washington had to send his farm products to Britain on British ships. British merchants sold his products in London. Washington had to buy goods in Britain with the money he made. Then, Washington's purchases were shipped back to Virginia.

While her husband was away from home, Martha Washington managed Mount Vernon's farms.

Washington did not like this arrangement. He thought the British took advantage of the colonists. He worried his farm products were being sold for less than they were worth. And, he believed he was charged too much for goods and transportation.

So Washington decided to sell his farm products elsewhere, such as the West Indies. And, he began to produce goods that he previously had to buy, such as cloth. Washington also added a grain mill and a commercial fishery to Mount Vernon.

Washington built Mount Vernon into a successful business. He expanded the plantation's lands and improved the house and gardens. And, he continued to work in the House of **Burgesses** passing laws for Virginia.

Washington's grain mill was very successful. Only Mount Vernon's farms and fishery made more money.

REBELLION

Britain had spent a lot of money fighting the **French and Indian War**. It also cost money to govern the American colonies and protect them from further attacks. The British parliament thought the colonists should help pay these costs.

To this end, parliament passed the **Stamp Act** in 1765. Washington and many other colonists opposed the act. They threatened to tar and feather the tax collectors! So, few tax collectors were willing to gather the money.

The Stamp Act was **repealed** on March 18, 1766. But, the British government still tried to raise money from the colonists. In 1767, parliament passed the **Townshend Acts**.

At this point, tensions in the colonies were high. On March 5, 1770, a mob of people gathered in Boston, Massachusetts. They threw snowballs at some British troops. The soldiers opened fire, killing five people. The event became known as the Boston Massacre.

Unrest in the colonies continued. In 1773, parliament passed the **Tea Act**. On December 26, colonists responded to this new act. Colonists dressed up as Mohawk Native Americans. Then, they climbed onto a ship in Boston Harbor. The ship had a cargo of tea that had been shipped from Britain. The colonists threw the tea into the ocean! This is called the Boston Tea Party.

Paul Revere painted this image of the Boston Massacre. On April 18, 1775, Revere would make his famous midnight ride to warn the colonists that the British were coming.

In response, parliament passed the **Coercive Acts** in 1774. Among other laws, these acts closed Boston's port and revoked the colony's **charter**. The colonists were so incensed that they called the laws the Intolerable Acts.

The colonists were losing their freedoms. They had to decide what to do. On September 5, 1774, representatives from all the colonies except Georgia met in Philadelphia, Pennsylvania. They called themselves the First Continental Congress. Washington attended as a representative from Virginia.

The Second Continental Congress met at Independence Hall in Philadelphia, Pennsylvania.

The men decided to **boycott** British goods. They forbade importing goods from Britain. They also rejected goods from other countries that were subject to British taxes. Soon after, the **American Revolution** began.

On May 10, 1775, representatives from all the colonies again met in Philadelphia. The Second Continental Congress adopted the Declaration of Independence on July 4, 1776. It said the colonies wanted to be free. The Congress also wrote the Articles of Confederation. This document joined the colonies as the United States of America.

The Second Continental Congress also created the Continental army. The representatives chose Washington to lead the army. Washington would lead the fight for independence from Britain.

The Declaration of Independence

REVOLUTION

On March 17, 1776, Washington's troops forced the British soldiers out of Boston. That summer, the British invaded New York. In September, Washington sent troops into Canada. They protected New York's northern border.

But on November 16, the British army captured Fort Washington on Manhattan Island. They killed many colonial soldiers. Washington and his men retreated from New York. They crossed New Jersey and into Pennsylvania.

Then, Washington made a daring move. On the night of December 25, he led his men across the Delaware River. They traveled through cold and snow to the British camp at Trenton, New Jersey. The British were so surprised that they lost the battle. A few days later, the colonists won another battle at Princeton.

But Washington's soldiers soon reached a low point. In autumn 1777, they lost two important battles in Pennsylvania at Brandywine and Germantown. They camped for the winter at Valley Forge. That winter was very cold. The soldiers did not have enough food or proper clothing. Many died from **exposure** and disease.

The colonists needed help, and the French came to their aid. In 1778, the French navy blocked New York Harbor. This kept the British from receiving supplies. Then in 1781, French soldiers helped the colonists win the Battle of Yorktown. On September 3, 1783, the British and the colonists signed the Treaty of Paris. The colonists had won the **American Revolution**.

Washington crossing the Delaware River

A NEW NATION

In 1783, Washington went home to Mount Vernon. He resigned his position in the army that December. He was glad to be home with his family.

But the United States had new problems. The Articles of Confederation did not give the federal government enough power. The United States could not collect taxes to pay its **debts**.

In 1787, leaders from each state gathered in Philadelphia. They held a meeting called the **Constitutional** Convention. They wanted to create a stronger set of laws for the United States. Washington was a delegate from Virginia.

The delegates picked Washington to be the convention's president. Together, they created the U.S. Constitution.

The U.S. Constitution is the supreme law of the land.

Washington holds the U.S. Constitution at the Constitutional Convention

Then, the new nation held its first presidential election. Washington received every electoral vote. He would soon become the first president of the United States.

THE FIRST PRESIDENT

Washington was **inaugurated** on April 30, 1789. His first task was to establish five executive departments. Washington then picked people to head these departments. These men became the first cabinet. These departments and the cabinet are still part of our government today.

At that time, the nation's capital moved around the country. It had been in New York City, New York, and Philadelphia, Pennsylvania. The United States needed the stability of a permanent capital. President Washington chose a location near the Potomac River. When it was finished, the capital city was named Washington, D.C., in honor of President Washington.

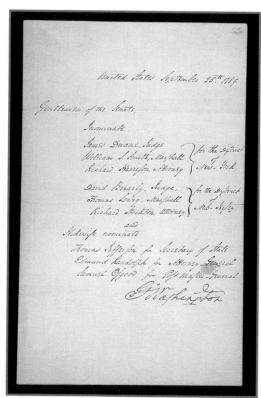

A letter from Washington to the U.S. Senate with district court and cabinet nominations

24

During his first term, President Washington created a financial plan for the country. He intended to pay all the nation's **debts**. Washington set up a money system based on gold and silver. And, he supported the creation of home businesses to end American dependence on imported British goods.

Washington helped create the federal court system. And in 1791, the states approved the **Bill of Rights**.

Thomas Jefferson served as secretary of state in Washington's cabinet. In 1801, Jefferson became the nation's third president.

In 1792, President Washington was elected to a second term. He signed laws that let the government raise money by taxation. He created a system of banks. They were allowed to issue paper money. But, citizens could exchange the paper money for gold or silver at the banks.

At this time, France was engaged in the **French Revolution**. France had helped America in its own war for independence. So, the French government now wanted the United States to help in return.

But President Washington would not help. He believed the United States was still too weak. He did not want to strain the resources of the new nation. In 1793, Washington issued the Statement of Neutrality. It said the United States would not take sides in the conflict.

Some people did not agree with the president's decision. Yet, many Americans wanted Washington to run for a third term. However, Washington did not think it was wise for a person to have such a powerful position for so long. In 1796, he went home to Mount Vernon. John Adams was elected the nation's second president.

SUPREME COURT APPOINTMENTS

JOHN JAY, JAMES WILSON - 1789
JOHN RUTLEDGE, WILLIAM CUSHING,
JOHN BLAIR, JAMES IREDELL - 1790
THOMAS JOHNSON - 1792
WILLIAM PATERSON - 1793
JOHN RUTLEDGE - 1795
SAMUEL CHASE, OLIVER ELLSWORTH - 1796

PRESIDENT WASHINGTON'S CABINET

FIRST TERM
APRIL 30, 1789–
MARCH 4, 1793

- **STATE –** Thomas Jefferson
- **TREASURY –** Alexander Hamilton
- **WAR –** Henry Knox
- **ATTORNEY GENERAL –** Edmund Randolph

SECOND TERM
MARCH 4, 1793–
MARCH 4, 1797

- **STATE –** Thomas Jefferson
  Edmund Randolph (from January 2, 1794)
  Timothy Pickering (from August 20, 1795)
- **TREASURY –** Alexander Hamilton
  Oliver Wolcott Jr. (from February 2, 1795)
- **WAR –** Henry Knox
  Timothy Pickering (from January 2, 1795)
  James McHenry (from February 6, 1796)
- **ATTORNEY GENERAL –** Edmund Randolph
  William Bradford (from January 29, 1794)
  Charles Lee (from December 10, 1795)

A PRIVATE CITIZEN

Washington was happy to be home with his family. While he was president, Washington's stepson, Jack, had died. So Washington and Martha adopted Jack's children, Eleanor and George. Now they were part of home life, too.

Troubles between the United States and France continued. In 1798, President Adams decided the United States needed a bigger army for national security. He asked Washington to help build the army. Washington worked to help plan the army. Then he returned to Mount Vernon.

One winter day, Washington rode his horse in heavy snow. He got cold and wet, and he became very sick. On December 14, 1799, George Washington died. People from all over the world mourned his death.

Washington was a skilled military leader. His ability to motivate troops led to the nation's independence. He helped create both the Declaration of Independence and the U.S. **Constitution**. As president, Washington worked to build a strong financial system.

This helped the country maintain its independence. For all this important work, George Washington is known as the Father of Our Country.

Gilbert Stuart painted this portrait of Washington. In 1814, First Lady Dolley Madison saved it when the British burned down the White House during the War of 1812.

OFFICE OF THE PRESIDENT

BRANCHES OF GOVERNMENT

The U.S. government is divided into three branches. They are the executive, legislative, and judicial branches. This division is called a separation of powers. Each branch has some power over the others. This is called a system of checks and balances.

EXECUTIVE BRANCH

The executive branch enforces laws. It is made up of the president, the vice president, and the president's cabinet. The president represents the United States around the world. He or she oversees relations with other countries and signs treaties. The president signs bills into law and appoints officials and federal judges. He or she also leads the military and manages government workers.

LEGISLATIVE BRANCH

The legislative branch makes laws, maintains the military, and regulates trade. It also has the power to declare war. This branch consists of the Senate and the House of Representatives. Together, these two houses make up Congress. Each state has two senators. A state's population determines the number of representatives it has.

JUDICIAL BRANCH

The judicial branch interprets laws. It consists of district courts, courts of appeals, and the Supreme Court. District courts try cases. If a person disagrees with a trial's outcome, he or she may appeal. If the courts of appeals support the ruling, a person may appeal to the Supreme Court. The Supreme Court also makes sure that laws follow the U.S. Constitution.

QUALIFICATIONS FOR OFFICE

To be president, a person must meet three requirements. A candidate must be at least 35 years old and a natural-born U.S. citizen. He or she must also have lived in the United States for at least 14 years.

ELECTORAL COLLEGE

The U.S. presidential election is an indirect election. Voters from each state choose electors to represent them in the Electoral College. The number of electors from each state is based on population. Each elector has one electoral vote. Electors are pledged to cast their vote for the candidate who receives the highest number of popular votes in their state. A candidate must receive the majority of Electoral College votes to win.

TERM OF OFFICE

Each president may be elected to two four-year terms. Sometimes, a president may only be elected once. This happens if he or she served more than two years of the previous president's term.

The presidential election is held on the Tuesday after the first Monday in November. The president is sworn in on January 20 of the following year. At that time, he or she takes the oath of office:

I do solemnly swear (or affirm) that I will faithfully execute the office of President of the United States, and will to the best of my ability, preserve, protect and defend the Constitution of the United States.

Line of Succession

The Presidential Succession Act of 1947 defines who becomes president if the president cannot serve. The vice president is first in the line of succession. Next are the Speaker of the House and the President Pro Tempore of the Senate. If none of these individuals is able to serve, the office falls to the president's cabinet members. They would take office in the order in which each department was created:

Secretary of State

Secretary of the Treasury

Secretary of Defense

Attorney General

Secretary of the Interior

Secretary of Agriculture

Secretary of Commerce

Secretary of Labor

Secretary of Health and Human Services

Secretary of Housing and Urban Development

Secretary of Transportation

Secretary of Energy

Secretary of Education

Secretary of Veterans Affairs

Secretary of Homeland Security

BENEFITS

• While in office, the president receives a salary of $400,000 each year. He or she lives in the White House and has 24-hour Secret Service protection.

• The president may travel on a Boeing 747 jet called Air Force One. The airplane can accommodate 70 passengers. It has kitchens, a dining room, sleeping areas, and a conference room. It also has fully equipped offices with the latest communications systems. Air Force One can fly halfway around the world before needing to refuel. It can even refuel in flight!

• If the president wishes to travel by car, he or she uses Cadillac One. Cadillac One is a Cadillac Deville. It has been modified with heavy armor and communications systems. The president takes Cadillac One along when visiting other countries if secure transportation will be needed.

• The president also travels on a helicopter called Marine One. Like the presidential car, Marine One accompanies the president when traveling abroad if necessary.

• Sometimes, the president needs to get away and relax with family and friends. Camp David is the official presidential retreat. It is located in the cool, wooded mountains in Maryland. The U.S. Navy maintains the retreat, and the U.S. Marine Corps keeps it secure. The camp offers swimming, tennis, golf, and hiking.

• When the president leaves office, he or she receives Secret Service protection for ten more years. He or she also receives a yearly pension of $191,300 and funding for office space, supplies, and staff.

PRESIDENTS AND THEIR TERMS

PRESIDENT	PARTY	TOOK OFFICE	LEFT OFFICE	TERMS SERVED	VICE PRESIDENT
George Washington	None	April 30, 1789	March 4, 1797	Two	John Adams
John Adams	Federalist	March 4, 1797	March 4, 1801	One	Thomas Jefferson
Thomas Jefferson	Democratic-Republican	March 4, 1801	March 4, 1809	Two	Aaron Burr, George Clinton
James Madison	Democratic-Republican	March 4, 1809	March 4, 1817	Two	George Clinton, Elbridge Gerry
James Monroe	Democratic-Republican	March 4, 1817	March 4, 1825	Two	Daniel D. Tompkins
John Quincy Adams	Democratic-Republican	March 4, 1825	March 4, 1829	One	John C. Calhoun
Andrew Jackson	Democrat	March 4, 1829	March 4, 1837	Two	John C. Calhoun, Martin Van Buren
Martin Van Buren	Democrat	March 4, 1837	March 4, 1841	One	Richard M. Johnson
William H. Harrison	Whig	March 4, 1841	April 4, 1841	Died During First Term	John Tyler
John Tyler	Whig	April 6, 1841	March 4, 1845	Completed Harrison's Term	Office Vacant
James K. Polk	Democrat	March 4, 1845	March 4, 1849	One	George M. Dallas
Zachary Taylor	Whig	March 5, 1849	July 9, 1850	Died During First Term	Millard Fillmore

34

PRESIDENT	PARTY	TOOK OFFICE	LEFT OFFICE	TERMS SERVED	VICE PRESIDENT
Millard Fillmore	Whig	July 10, 1850	March 4, 1853	Completed Taylor's Term	Office Vacant
Franklin Pierce	Democrat	March 4, 1853	March 4, 1857	One	William R.D. King
James Buchanan	Democrat	March 4, 1857	March 4, 1861	One	John C. Breckinridge
Abraham Lincoln	Republican	March 4, 1861	April 15, 1865	Served One Term, Died During Second Term	Hannibal Hamlin, Andrew Johnson
Andrew Johnson	Democrat	April 15, 1865	March 4, 1869	Completed Lincoln's Second Term	Office Vacant
Ulysses S. Grant	Republican	March 4, 1869	March 4, 1877	Two	Schuyler Colfax, Henry Wilson
Rutherford B. Hayes	Republican	March 3, 1877	March 4, 1881	One	William A. Wheeler
James A. Garfield	Republican	March 4, 1881	September 19, 1881	Died During First Term	Chester Arthur
Chester Arthur	Republican	September 20, 1881	March 4, 1885	Completed Garfield's Term	Office Vacant
Grover Cleveland	Democrat	March 4, 1885	March 4, 1889	One	Thomas A. Hendricks
Benjamin Harrison	Republican	March 4, 1889	March 4, 1893	One	Levi P. Morton
Grover Cleveland	Democrat	March 4, 1893	March 4, 1897	One	Adlai E. Stevenson
William McKinley	Republican	March 4, 1897	September 14, 1901	Served One Term, Died During Second Term	Garret A. Hobart, Theodore Roosevelt

PRESIDENT	PARTY	TOOK OFFICE	LEFT OFFICE	TERMS SERVED	VICE PRESIDENT
Theodore Roosevelt	Republican	September 14, 1901	March 4, 1909	Completed McKinley's Second Term, Served One Term	Office Vacant, Charles Fairbanks
William Taft	Republican	March 4, 1909	March 4, 1913	One	James S. Sherman
Woodrow Wilson	Democrat	March 4, 1913	March 4, 1921	Two	Thomas R. Marshall
Warren G. Harding	Republican	March 4, 1921	August 2, 1923	Died During First Term	Calvin Coolidge
Calvin Coolidge	Republican	August 3, 1923	March 4, 1929	Completed Harding's Term, Served One Term	Office Vacant, Charles Dawes
Herbert Hoover	Republican	March 4, 1929	March 4, 1933	One	Charles Curtis
Franklin D. Roosevelt	Democrat	March 4, 1933	April 12, 1945	Served Three Terms, Died During Fourth Term	John Nance Garner, Henry A. Wallace, Harry S. Truman
Harry S. Truman	Democrat	April 12, 1945	January 20, 1953	Completed Roosevelt's Fourth Term, Served One Term	Office Vacant, Alben Barkley
Dwight D. Eisenhower	Republican	January 20, 1953	January 20, 1961	Two	Richard Nixon
John F. Kennedy	Democrat	January 20, 1961	November 22, 1963	Died During First Term	Lyndon B. Johnson
Lyndon B. Johnson	Democrat	November 22, 1963	January 20, 1969	Completed Kennedy's Term, Served One Term	Office Vacant, Hubert H. Humphrey
Richard Nixon	Republican	January 20, 1969	August 9, 1974	Completed First Term, Resigned During Second Term	Spiro T. Agnew, Gerald Ford

PRESIDENT	PARTY	TOOK OFFICE	LEFT OFFICE	TERMS SERVED	VICE PRESIDENT
Gerald Ford	Republican	August 9, 1974	January 20, 1977	Completed Nixon's Second Term	Nelson A. Rockefeller
Jimmy Carter	Democrat	January 20, 1977	January 20, 1981	One	Walter Mondale
Ronald Reagan	Republican	January 20, 1981	January 20, 1989	Two	George H.W. Bush
George H.W. Bush	Republican	January 20, 1989	January 20, 1993	One	Dan Quayle
Bill Clinton	Democrat	January 20, 1993	January 20, 2001	Two	Al Gore
George W. Bush	Republican	January 20, 2001	January 20, 2009	Two	Dick Cheney
Barack Obama	Democrat	January 20, 2009			Joe Biden

"To be prepared for war is one of the most effectual means of preserving peace." George Washington

WRITE TO THE PRESIDENT

You may write to the president at:

**The White House
1600 Pennsylvania Avenue NW
Washington, DC 20500**

You may e-mail the president at:
comments@whitehouse.gov

GLOSSARY

ambush - to conduct a surprise attack from a hidden position.

American Revolution - from 1775 to 1783. A war for independence between Great Britain and its North American colonies. The colonists won and created the United States of America.

Bill of Rights - the first 10 amendments to the U.S. Constitution. They guarantee basic rights and freedoms to all citizens.

boycott - to refuse to deal with a person, a store, or an organization until they agree to certain conditions.

burgess - a representative in a colonial government.

charter - a written contract that states a colony's boundaries and form of government.

Coercive Acts - five laws passed in 1774. They were intended to punish Massachusetts colonists for the Boston Tea Party and to strengthen British authority in the colony.

Constitution - the laws that govern the United States. Something relating to or following the laws of a constitution is constitutional.

cooper - a person who makes or repairs wooden barrels or tubs.

cultivated - improved by education or training.

debt - something owed to someone, usually money.

exposure - being unprotected from severe weather.

French and Indian War - from 1754 to 1763. A series of battles fought for control of land in North America. England and its colonies fought against France, its colonies, and several Native American tribes.

French Revolution - revolutionary movement in France between 1787 and 1799.

inaugurate - (ih-NAW-gyuh-rayt) - to swear into a political office.

mentor - a guide who serves as a good example.

repeal - to formally withdraw or cancel.

Stamp Act - a law passed in 1765. It taxed all North American colonial commercial and legal papers, newspapers, pamphlets, cards, almanacs, and dice.

survey - to measure the size, the shape, and the position of an area of land or a feature on that land. A surveyor is a person who surveys.

Tea Act - a law passed in 1773. It lowered taxes on tea sold by the British East India Company.

Townshend Acts - four laws passed in 1767. One charged tax on imports to the North American colonies on common goods such as paper, paint, lead, glass, and tea.

will - a legal declaration of a person's wishes regarding the disposal of his or her property after death.

WEB SITES

To learn more about George Washington, visit ABDO Publishing Company on the World Wide Web at **www.abdopublishing.com**. Web sites about George Washington are featured on our Book Links page. These links are routinely monitored and updated to provide the most current information available.

INDEX